20 QUESTIONS

WHY DO FEET SmelL?

By Gilda & Melvin Berger

And **20** answers about the human body

SCHOLASTIC INC.

NEW YORK • TORONTO • LONDON • AUCKLAND
SYDNEY • MEXICO CITY • NEW DELHI • HONG KONG

Text copyright © 2012 by Gilda & Melvin Berger
All rights reserved. Published by Scholastic Inc., *Publishers since 1920.*
SCHOLASTIC and associated logos are trademarks and/or registered trademarks of Scholastic Inc.

ISBN 978-0-545-34665-8

10 9 8 7 6 5 4 3 2 1   12 13 14 15 16

Printed in the U.S.A.   40
First edition, February 2012
Book design by Kay Petronio

Q

Why do noses run?

Noses are moist and run a little bit almost all the time.

The stuff that forms in your nose is called mucus. It is sticky and catches dirt or germs that you breathe in. The mucus keeps these things from getting into your lungs. From time to time, some **germs** or **viruses** do get through. Viruses can cause a cold. A cold can make the lining of your nose produce even more mucus. It may even make the mucus look yellow or green—until you're well again.

Q What's a burp?

5

A burp is mostly a bubble of air that comes up from your stomach.

It passes through your throat and out of your mouth with a loud *pop*. Oops—excuse *me*! You usually burp after eating. A burp can be air that you swallowed because you ate too fast or gulped your food. Or it can be gas from something you drank, such as bubbly soda. The bubbles need to escape, and out they come as a burp. To burp is human; to cover your mouth is polite.

Q Why do feet smell?

Your feet smell because they sweat.

Sweat, by itself, is little more than salty water. It does not smell. But the sweat on your feet soaks into your socks and shoes. When your feet are hot, you sweat even more. This makes a real feast for the germs that are already normally on your feet. The germs grow and multiply and make your feet smell!

Q Do you sneeze in your sleep?

No! No one sneezes when asleep.

That's because the **nerves** that make you sneeze go to sleep when you do. When you're awake, you sneeze when something tickles your nose or you have a cold. The cause of the tickle can be anything from a tiny bit of dirt, dust, or **pollen** to **bacteria** or viruses. The nerves in your nose signal your brain to get rid of it. Your brain flashes a message to your chest **muscles** to squeeze and send out a burst of air. *KACHOO!*

Q What good are eyebrows?

Eyebrows are more important than you may think.

Their job is to protect your sight by blocking things that might fall, blow, or drip into your eyes. Sweat, dirt, rain, or foreign objects can seriously damage delicate parts of the eye. Eyebrows also help show your feelings. Try expressing anger, fear, surprise, or confusion without moving your eyebrows.

Q Where do freckles come from?

13

Freckles are
clumps of ta
or light brow
cells that forr
on your skin.

Most freckles stay small. But some overlap and run together, making larger freckles. They seem to be due mostly to **heredity** and skin type. Spending lots of hours in the sun sometimes makes new freckles appear or old freckles grow darker. But luckily, if you don't like having freckles, they do not last forever. They often fade as you grow older.

Q Why does hair turn gray?

15

Some parents jok
that their kids ca
make their hair
turn gray!

Of course, that's not true. Hair gets its color from a substance found in skin, hair, and eyes called melanin. Melanin forms in the body before you are born to make your hair black, brown, blond, or red. As you grow older, your body makes less melanin. Without melanin, the hair loses all of its color and you're left with hair that is gray, white, or silver.

Q Can you ride a charley horse?

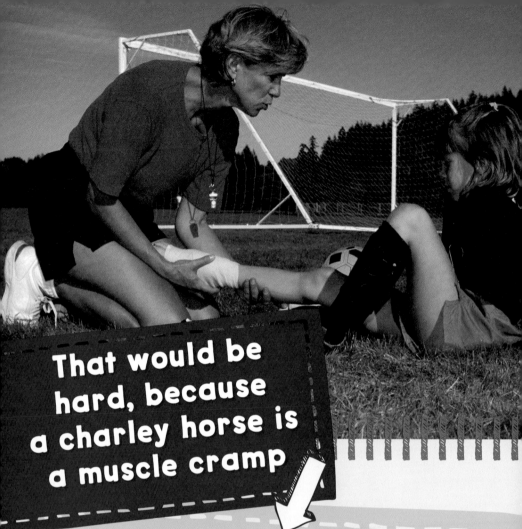

That would be hard, because a charley horse is a muscle cramp

Most often you get a cramp in a leg muscle. It may be caused by a blow to your leg, such as a kick during a soccer game, or from using your muscles a lot. The name may have come from a baseball player, Charles "Old Hoss" Radbourn, who got a cramp during a game in the 1880s. Seeing him limp, another player yelled out, "What's the matter with you, Charley Hoss?" Perhaps from then on, a leg cramp became known as a charley horse.

Q Why are lips red?

Tiny blood vessels under your skin make your lips look red.

The **blood vessels** are filled with bright red blood. The red color shows through since the blood vessels are close to the surface and the skin is very thin. In cold weather, the blood vessels move deeper beneath the skin. This makes the lips look slightly blue! Only humans have a red outline around the lips called the vermillion border.

Q Are yawns contagious?

Yes, most people yawn when they see someone else yawning.

No one is sure why humans and some animals yawn. Most experts agree that it happens when you are tired, sleepy, or bored. Yawning may be a way to stretch the muscles of your mouth and jaw. It may even be a way to get more **oxygen** into your body. Whatever the reason, when you see someone yawn, you often do the same!

Q

Why do you blink?

Blinking keeps your eyes clean and moist.

You usually open and shut your eyes automatically, without even deciding to do so. And blinking does not interfere with your vision at all. But sometimes you also blink on purpose. Something gets under an eyelid. You're blinded by a bright light. Or you're afraid that something—such as a ball, raindrop, or blowing sand— might hit or get into your eye. So, you blink.

Q What gives you goose bumps?

You get goose bumps when you are cold

You may also get goose bumps from a scary movie, TV show, or story. Being lost, frightened, or in a fight are other causes of goose bumps. The muscles attached to the hairs on your skin **contract** and pull the hairs up, making tiny bumps. If you look closely, you'll see a tiny hair in the center of each goose bump.

Q Why does your stomach growl?

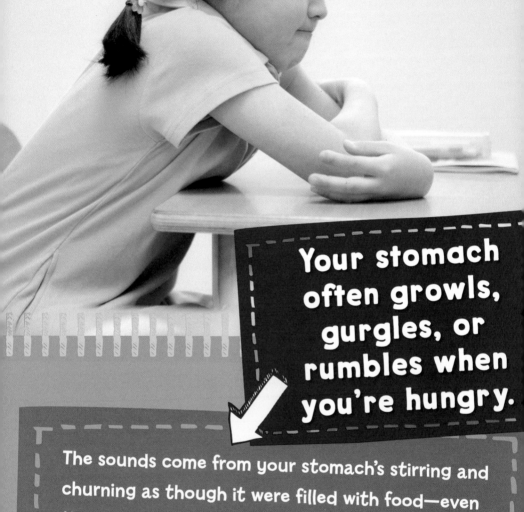

Your stomach often growls, gurgles, or rumbles when you're hungry.

The sounds come from your stomach's stirring and churning as though it were filled with food—even though it's empty! Your stomach may also growl after you eat. These sounds are made by the food passing through to your **intestines**. Sometimes just thinking of food can make your stomach growl. In a quiet room, it can be very embarrassing!

Q What's that stuff in your ears?

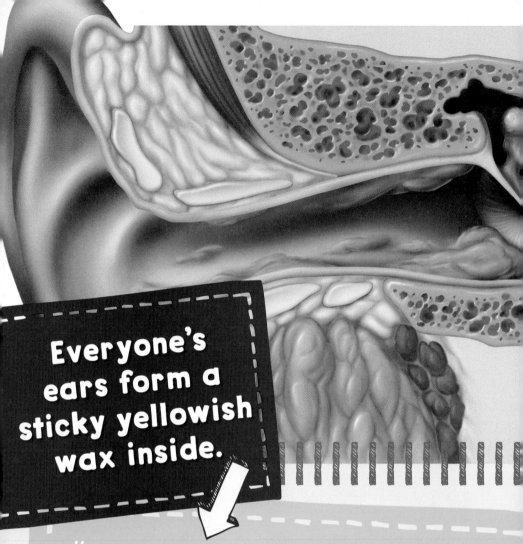

Everyone's ears form a sticky yellowish wax inside.

Its purpose is to keep the ears clean. The wax traps or blocks anything that flies, crawls, drips, or blows into the ear. This includes dust, dirt, mold, bugs, and water. Earwax also kills some germs. Too much earwax can hurt or make it hard to hear. Usually the wax makes its way to the ear opening and dries up. Then it either falls out or is removed when you wash your face.

110	15-5-2011
103	15-1-2011
97	7-6-2010
91	20-2-2010
84	8-8-2009

Indeed you are!

Every morning, you are a tiny bit taller than when you went to sleep. This is because the bones in your **spine** spread a little apart while you're asleep. After you wake up and get out of bed, you get busy. All day long, you work and play. The pull of **gravity** and the weight of your body push the bones of your spine together. You become a little shorter. But don't worry. You'll be taller the next morning!

Q What makes you blush?

If you're like other people, you mostly blush when you feel embarrassed.

But you also blush when you're ashamed, angry, or shy. Blushing makes your face turn slightly pink or red. The color comes from blood vessels beneath the skin of your face that widen and fill with more blood than usual. The red blood adds color to your face.

Q Why does skin wrinkle in water?

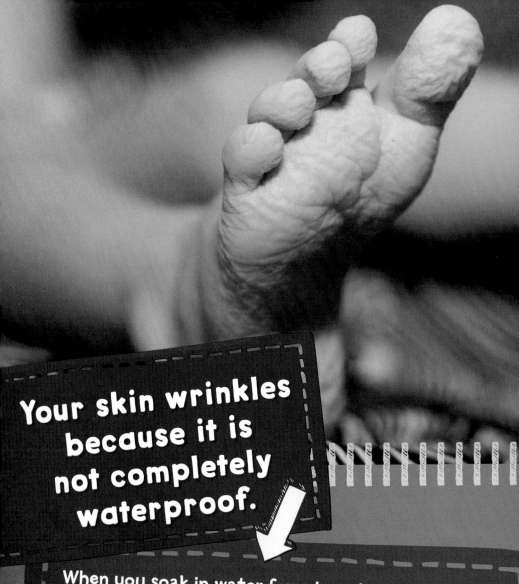

Your skin wrinkles because it is not completely waterproof.

When you soak in water for a long time—while you're swimming or bathing—some water gets into the outer layer of skin. The outside of your skin swells with the extra water, which makes the wrinkles. But your skin doesn't swell evenly. Some places wrinkle more than others. The skin of your fingers and toes, for example, shows the most wrinkles. That's because the skin here is very thick.

Q Which is the strongest muscle in your body?

The stronges muscle, for it size, is your tongue!

Just try to chew, swallow, talk, or sing without using it. We bet you can't! The tongue has to be very strong to do all of these things. The tongue is also the most movable **organ** in the body. It is made up of several small muscles that let it move in many different ways.

Q Why do you have a belly button?

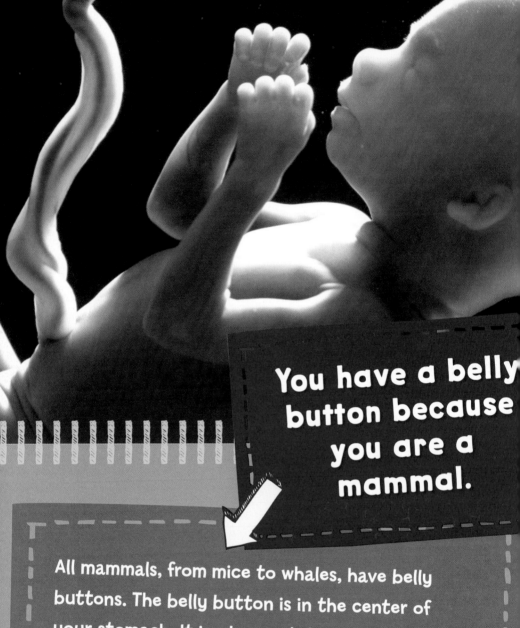

You have a belly button because you are a mammal.

All mammals, from mice to whales, have belly buttons. The belly button is in the center of your stomach. It is where a tube attached you to your mother before you were born. The tube, or umbilical cord, brought you food and oxygen before you could eat and breathe on your own.

Q What's a funny bone?

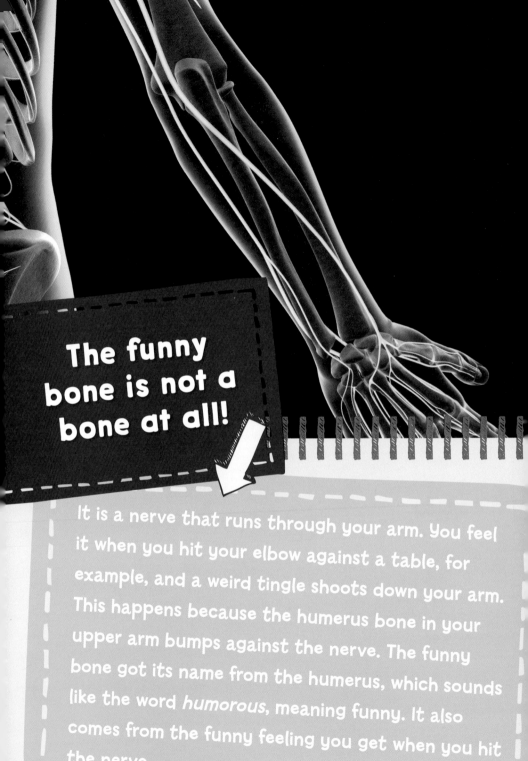

The funny bone is not a bone at all!

It is a nerve that runs through your arm. You feel it when you hit your elbow against a table, for example, and a weird tingle shoots down your arm. This happens because the humerus bone in your upper arm bumps against the nerve. The funny bone got its name from the humerus, which sounds like the word *humorous*, meaning funny. It also comes from the funny feeling you get when you hit the nerve.

20 BONUS FACTS

1 The average person produces about 4 cups (0.9 L) of mucus inside the nose every day.

2 In some countries, such as China, burping means you enjoyed a meal.

3 Men's feet sweat more than women's do.

4 You can't sneeze with your eyes open!

5 The bones under your eyebrows make little ledges that also protect your eyes.

6 Most freckles appear on the face and hands.

7 Beards are the fastest-growing hairs on the human body.

8 The best way to treat a charley horse is to rub or stretch the muscle.

9 The average woman swallows about 6 pounds (2.7 kg) of lipstick in her lifetime.

10 An average yawn lasts about six seconds.

11 You blink about fifteen times a minute.

12 You hardly ever get goose bumps on your face.

13 Doctors call stomach growls borborygmi.

14 Doctors say that you should never put anything smaller than your elbow into your ear.

15 You can lose as much as 1 inch (2.5 cm) of height during the day.

16 Few people blush before the age of two.

17 Skin that wrinkles in water quickly returns to normal.

18 The tip of your tongue is one of the most sensitive parts of your body.

19 Another name for your belly button is *navel*.

20 The funny bone nerve in your elbow runs from your little finger to your brain.

GLOSSARY

Bacteria - microscopic living things that exist everywhere and can either be useful or harmful

Blood vessel - any of the tubes in your body through which blood flows

Contract - to tighten

Germ - a tiny living organism that can cause disease

Gravity - the force that pulls things toward the center of the earth

Heredity - the process of passing traits from a parent to a child before the child is born

Intestine - a long tube in the body below the stomach that helps digests food

Mammal - a warm-blooded animal that has hair or fur and usually gives birth to live babies

Muscle - a type of tissue in the body that can pull on bones to move parts of the body

Nerve - a fiber that carries messages between the brain and other parts of the body

Organ - a part of the body, such as the heart or kidneys, that has a certain purpose

Oxygen - a colorless gas found in air and water that is important for most forms of life

Pollen - tiny grains produced by flowers

Spine - the backbone of the body

Viruses - very tiny organisms (smaller than bacteria) that grow inside living cells and can cause disease

INDEX